If You Feel Blue, Get on Your Ski-doo

and Other Poems

If You Feel Blue, Get on Your Ski-doo
and Other Poems

Text: Various
Publishers: Tania Mazzeo and Eliza Webb
Series consultant: Amanda Sutera
    Hands on Heads Consulting
Poem compilation: Jarrah Moore
Editor: Jarrah Moore
Project editor: Annabel Smith
Designer: Jess Kelly
Project designer: Danielle Maccarone
Illustrations: Soia Di Chiara Manetti,
    Andy Catling, Sara Ugolotti,
    Felishia Henditirto
Permissions researcher: Debbie Gallagher
Production controller: Renee Tome

Acknowledgements
'If You Feel Blue, Get on Your Ski-doo': In
Southern Convergence: Antarctic Art
(Pemmican Press, 2000) © Margaret
Mahy, with permission via Watson, Little;
'The Saw-see': From https:
//australianchildrenspoetry.com.
au/2023/03/23/the-saw-see-by-james-
aitchison; 'Stick Insect': In Cloud Soup (The
Emma Press, 2021); 'Clouds': In It's the
Sound of the Thing by Maxine Beneba
Clarke (Hardie Grant Children's
Publishing, 2023); 'Ocean Rhythms': In
Splash!: Poems of Our Watery World
(Orchard Books, Scholastic Inc., 2002);
'How awkward while playing with glue': In
I'm Going To Pet a Worm Today (Margaret
McElderry Books, Simon & Schuster,
1991); 'On Your Marks': From https:
//jennyerlanger.com/poems/on-your-
marks; 'A Football Game': In Instructor
magazine, November 1960 © 1960
Scholastic Inc. Reprinted by permission of
Scholastic Inc.; 'Fog': In Chicago Poems
(Henry Holt, 1916); 'Grandpa, Me and
Poetry': From Grandpa, Me and Poetry by
Sally Morgan and Craig Smith (Omnibus
Books, Scholastic Australia, 2018). Text ©
Sally Morgan, 2018. Reproduced with
permission from Scholastic Australia; 'The
Island': In When We Were Very Young
(Methuen & Co., 1924); 'Bluebottle': In
Storm's Eye (Oxford University Press,
1992), © Judith Nicholls 1992, by
permission of the author; 'Sir Smasham
Upp': © E.V. Rieu (1933), in The Flattered
Flying Fish and Other Poems (Dutton,
1962); 'Russian Doll': In The Language of
Cat and Other Poems © Rachel Rooney
2011 (Frances Lincoln Books), reproduced
by permission of David Higham
Associates; 'The Secret Place': In The Ice
Cream Store (HarperCollins Canada,
2013); 'Urban Forests': Published by Red
Room Poetry, https://redroompoetry.
org/poets/jeanine-leane/urban-forests.

Illustrations © 2024 Cengage Learning Australia Pty Limited

Copyright Notice
This Work is copyright. No part of this Work may be reproduced, stored
in a retrieval system, or transmitted in any form or by any means
without prior written permission of the Publisher. Except as permitted
under the Copyright Act 1968, for example any fair dealing for the
purposes of private study, research, criticism or review, subject to
certain limitations. These limitations include: Restricting the copying to a
maximum of one chapter or 10% of this book, whichever is greater;
Providing an appropriate notice and warning with the copies of the
Work disseminated; Taking all reasonable steps to limit access to these
copies to people authorised to receive these copies; Ensuring you hold
the appropriate Licences issued by the Copyright Agency Limited ("CAL"),
supply a remuneration notice to CAL and pay any required fees.

ISBN 978 0 17 033437 2

Cengage Learning Australia
Level 5, 80 Dorcas Street
Southbank VIC 3006 Australia
Phone: 1300 790 853
Email: aust.nelsonprimary@cengage.com

For learning solutions, visit cengage.com.au

Printed in China by 1010 Printing International Ltd
1 2 3 4 5 6 7 28 27 26 25 24

*Nelson acknowledges the Traditional Owners and Custodians
of the lands of all First Nations Peoples. We pay respect
to Elders past and present, and extend that respect to
all First Nations Peoples today.*

NovaStar

Contents

If You Feel Blue, Get on Your Ski-doo

If you feel blue, get on your ski-doo
And swiffle your way through the snow.
Ski-dare to be bold even though it is cold!
Ski-don't let it lay you low!

Ski-daddle along, singing a song,
Ski-do what has got to be done!
Your heart will ski-dance at each fabulous chance,
And ski-dart with delight at the fun.

Margaret Mahy

The Saw-see

Once I had a seesaw
That lifted me up high.
I saw across my neighbours,
Right up into the sky.

My seasaw let me see so far
I saw the distant sea,
So now I call my seesaw
A seesawsawseasee!

James Aitchison

Stick Insect

Twig twitcher,
leaf creeper,
nobbly gobbler
of secret greens.

The one with the goggly eyes
whose disguise
relies
on being mostly unsurprising.

Spiny climber,
motionless muncher,
stickler for a really good
stick.

Stem statue,
I salute you.

Kate Wakeling

Clouds

Curling across clear blue sky.

Lazy powder-puff white,

Over rustling treetops,

Under blistering hot sun.

Drifting,

Silently, away.

Maxine Beneba Clarke

Ocean Rhythms

Wave after wave
each wave
a beat
each beat
repeating
each stretch
receding.
This is Earth's
old wild heart
beating.

Constance Levy

How awkward while playing with glue

How awkward while playing with glue
To suddenly find out that you
   Have stuck nice and tight
   Your left hand to your right
In a permanent how-do-you-do!

Constance Levy

On Your Marks

I've turned into jelly.
I don't have the strength.
My stomach is stuck in my throat.
Why did I say I could swim a whole length?
I don't even know how to float.

My goggles are loose,
Should have tightened the strap.
What if they happen to leak?
And what if my bathers just suddenly snap?
I'll be laughed at the rest of the week.

What if I don't make the end of the race?
What if I give up all hope?
I'll never be able to lift up my face
If I have to hold onto the rope.

My stomach is churning,
I'm still feeling bad,
I'm freezing ... and there goes the gun!

I'm kicking,
I'm splashing,
I'm swimming like mad.
Will I make it?
I have!
And I've won!

Jenny Erlanger

A Football Game

It's the might, it's the fight
Of two teams who won't give in –
It's the roar of the crowd
And the "Go, fight, win!"

It's the bands, it's the stands,
It's the colour everywhere.
It's the whiff, it's the sniff
Of popcorn on the air.

It's a thrill, it's a chill,
It's a cheer and then a sigh;
It's that deep, breathless hush
When the ball soars high.

Yes, it's more than a score,
Or a desperate grasp at fame;
Fun is King, win or lose –
That's a football game.

Alice Van Eck

Fog

The fog comes
on little cat feet.

It sits looking
over harbour and city
on silent haunches
and then moves on.

Carl Sandburg

Grandpa, Me and Poetry

When he laughs, he laughs loud
Like a horn blasting through the fog
   Or the magical barking of a midnight dog
      When I cry, I cry soft
Like a cloud whispering goodbye
   Or the silvery sighing of a starlit sky
      Grandpa is the sun, laughing with the light
I am the moon, kissing him goodnight.

Sally Morgan

The Island

If I had a ship,
I'd sail my ship,
I'd sail my ship
Through Eastern seas;
Down to a beach where the slow waves thunder –
The green curls over and the white falls under –
Boom! Boom! Boom!
On the sun-bright sand.
Then I'd leave my ship and I'd land,
And climb the steep white sand,
And climb to the trees,
The six dark trees,
The coco-nut trees on the cliff's green crown –

Hands and knees
To the coco-nut trees,
Face to the cliff as the stones patter down,
Up, up, up, staggering, stumbling,
Round the corner where the rock is crumbling,
Round this shoulder,
Over this boulder,
Up to the top where the six trees stand ....

And there would I rest, and lie,
My chin in my hands, and gaze
At the dazzle of sand below,
And the green waves curling slow
And the grey-blue distant haze
Where the sea goes up to the sky ....

And I'd say to myself as I looked so lazily down
    at the sea:
"There's nobody else in the world, and the world
    was made for me."

A. A. Milne

Bluebottle

Who dips, dives,
swoops out of space,
a buzz in his wings
and sky on his face;
now caught in the light,
now gone without trace,
a sliver of glass,
never still in one place?

Who's elusive as pickpocket,
lord of the flies;
who moves like a rocket,
bound for the skies?
Who's catapult, aeroplane,
always full-throttle?
Sky-diver, Jumping Jack,
comet, *bluebottle*!

Judith Nicholls

Sir Smasham Uppe

Good afternoon, Sir Smasham Uppe!
We're having tea: do take a cup.
Sugar and milk? Now let me see –
Two lumps, I think? … Good gracious me!
The silly thing slipped off your knee!
Pray don't apologise, old chap:
A very trivial mishap!
So clumsy of you? How absurd!
My dear Sir Smasham, not a word!
Now do sit down and have another,
And tell us all about your brother –
You know, the one who broke his head.
Is the poor fellow still in bed? –
A chair – allow me, sir! … Great Scott!
That *was* a nasty smash! Eh, what?
Oh, not at all: the chair was old –
Queen Anne, or so we have been told.
We've got at least a dozen more:
Just leave the pieces on the floor.

I want you to admire our view:
Come nearer to the window, do;
And look how beautiful … Tut, tut!
You didn't see that it was shut?
I hope you are not badly cut!
Not hurt? A fortunate escape!
Amazing! Not a single scrape!
And now, if you have finished tea,
I fancy you might like to see
A little thing or two I've got.
That china plate? Yes, worth a lot:
A beauty too … Ah, there it goes!
I trust it didn't hurt your toes?
Your elbow brushed it off the shelf?
Of course: I've done the same myself.
And now, my dear Sir Smasham – Oh,
You surely don't intend to go?
You *must* be off? Well, come again.
So glad you're fond of porcelain!

E. V. Rieu

Russian Doll

All you see is outside me: my painted smile,
the rosy-posy shell, the fluttery eyes.
A butter-won't-melt-in-my-mouth-type me.

But inside there's another me, bored till playtime.
The wasting paper, daytime dreamer.
A can't-be-bothered-sort-of me.

And inside there's another me, full of cheek.
The quick, slick joker with a poking tongue.
A class-clown-funny-one-of me.

And inside there's another me who's smaller, scared.
The scurrying, worrying, yes miss whisperer.
A wouldn't-say-boo-to-a-goosey me.

And inside there's another me, all cross and bothered.
The scowling hot-head, stamping feet.
A didn't-do-it-blameless me.

And inside there's another me, forever jealous,
who never gets enough, compared.
A grass-is-always-greener me.

And deepest down, kept secretly,
a tiny, solid skittle doll.
The girl that hides inside of me.

Rachel Rooney

The Secret Place

There's a place I go, inside myself,
    Where nobody else can be,
And none of my friends can tell it's there –
    Nobody knows but me.

It's hard to explain the way it feels,
    Or even where I go.
It isn't a place in time or space,
    But once I'm there, I *know*.

It's tiny, it's shiny, it can't be seen,
    But it's big as the sky at night …
I try to explain and it hurts my brain,
    But once I'm there, it's *right*.

There's a place I know inside myself,
    And it's neither big nor small,
And whenever I go, it feels as though
    I never left at all.

Dennis Lee

Urban Forests

growing strong without notice
weathering each season
sheltering strangers shading streets
anchored deep reaching high
standing still always moving

Jeanine Leane